"E" Is for Explorers

by Annalisa McMorrow
illustrated by Marilynn G. Barr

Dedicated to John Howland.

Publisher: Roberta Suid
Design & Production: Standing Watch Productions
Cover Design: David Hale

ISBN 1-57612-151-8

Printed in the United States of America
987654321

Contents

Introduction

E Is for Explorers is a month-long unit filled with informative and exciting cross-curriculum activities. Exploration-related history, language, math, art, spelling, homework, and game activities are featured for each week. Songs are also included.

Use the "Explorer Facts" (p. 6) to introduce the unit. This sheet features routes taken by several of the famous explorers featured in this resource book. Then help children make their Explorer Portfolios. They can use these to store all of their exploration-related activities, or to take materials home to share with their families.

Patterns throughout the unit can serve many purposes. For instance, some will work for use as name tags, or desk or cubby labels. You can also enlarge patterns to use as bulletin board decorations.

The activities in *E Is for Explorers* are intended for grades one through three. Some lessons may easily be simplified for younger children. For instance, if children cannot write their own reports or stories, they can dictate them to the teacher or teacher's helper, record them on a tape recorder for an audio report, or draw pictures to represent the words.

Graphic organizers and helpful patterns accompany several activities. These forms help the children to stay focused on the topics that they are researching or learning about.

The unit ends with a final game that allows children to share the knowledge that they've learned over the four week unit. Once children have finished the game, give the students Explorer Diplomas (p. 64), to show that they have mastered the beginning concepts of exploration.

To extend the *E Is for Explorers* unit, look for exploration-related books to store in your reading corner. Challenge children to be on the lookout for mentions of explorers in books and magazines that they read on their own.

The Web is also good place to locate information. Remember, Web sites change with frequency. Always check the sites yourself before sharing them with the students.

Below are several books for teacher use. Gather facts and pictures to share with the students.

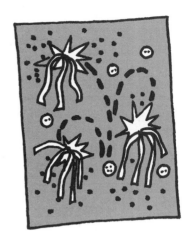

Explorer-related Books:

• *Lewis and Clark for Kids* by Janis Herbert (Chicago Review)
• *Marco Polo for Kids* by Janis Herbert (Chicago Review)
• *Sacagawea: Guide for the Lewis and Clark Expedition* by Hal Marcovitz (Chelsea House)
• *Stories from the Days of Christopher Columbus: A Multicultural Collection for Young Readers* by Alan Young, Judy Dockrey Young, Richard Young (August House)

Explorer Facts

Here are the routes taken by several famous explorers:

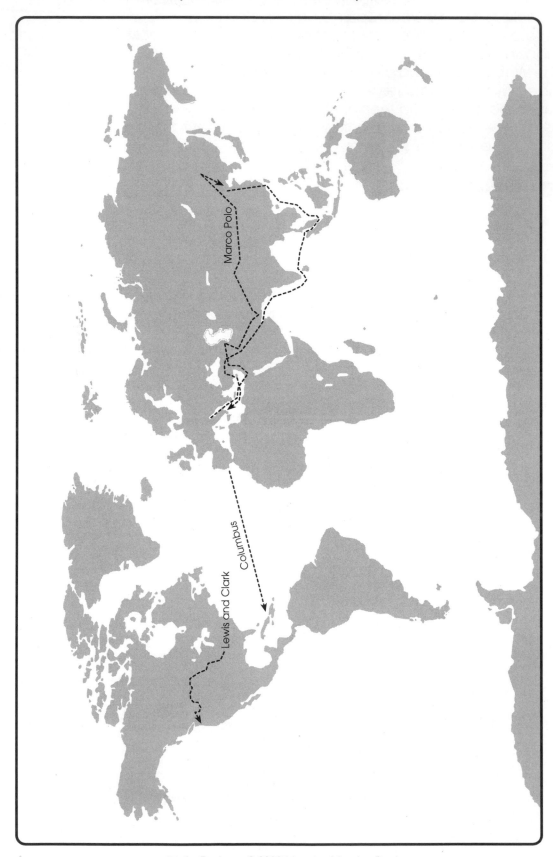

E Is for Explorers © 2002 Monday Morning Books

Explorer Portfolio

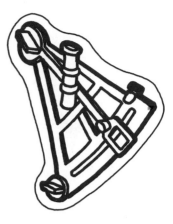

Materials:
Portfolio Patterns (p. 8), scissors, crayons or markers, glue, hole punch, yarn, legal-sized folders or large sheets of heavy construction paper

Preparation:
Duplicate a copy of the Portfolio Patterns for each child.

Directions:
1. Demonstrate how to make a portfolio. If using legal-sized folders, punch holes along the two open sides. Cut two arm-length pieces of yarn and tie knots in one side of each. Thread the yarn through the holes and tie the free ends together to make a strap. If using construction paper, fold the paper in half to make a folder, and then continue as described above.
2. Give each child a sheet of patterns to color and cut out.
3. Have the children decorate their portfolios with crayons, markers, and the patterns.

Options:
• The children can add their own hand-drawn pictures, as well. Or they can cut out pictures from magazines to glue to their portfolios.
• Provide old maps for the children to use to decorate their portfolios. (Ask for donations from home.)
• Cover the portfolios with contact paper for added sturdiness. Reinforce the holes with hole reinforcers.

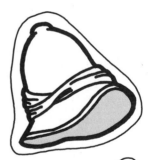

Portfolio Patterns

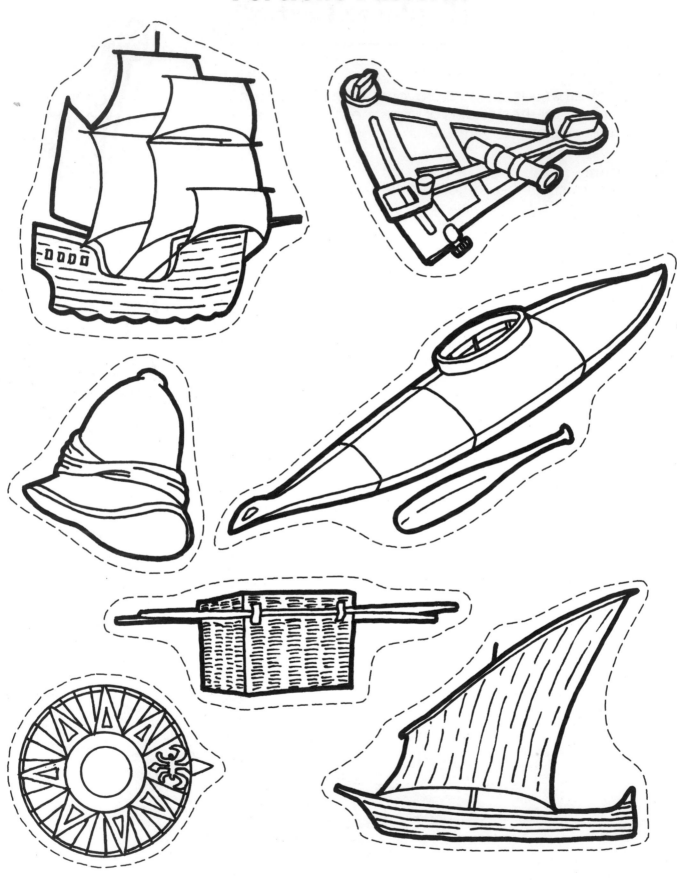

E Is for Explorers © 2002 Monday Morning Books

Marco Polo's Scrapbook

Marco Polo first traveled to China when he was 15 years old. During his journey, he paid attention to the amazing sights around him. The students, using the patterns provided, will create fictional scrapbooks for Marco Polo.

Materials:
Scrapbook Patterns (p. 10), crayons or markers, scissors, manila folders (one per child) or large sheets of construction paper, tape or glue

Preparation:
Duplicate a copy of the Scrapbook Patterns for each child.

Directions:
1. Discuss Marco Polo's journey and share books about the journey with the students.
2. Give each child a manila folder or a large sheet of construction paper to fold in half.
3. Have the children label the front of the folder "Marco Polo's Scrapbook."
4. Give each child the patterns to color, cut out, and glue inside the folders to make scrapbooks.
5. Children can add facts about Marco Polo to their folders. They can also add their own drawings of what Polo saw on his journey.

Scrapbook Patterns

Marco Polo was fascinated by different plants, animals, objects and inventions that he saw on his journeys. These included:

E Is for Explorers © 2002 Monday Morning Books

I'm Marco Polo

After returning to Venice, Marco Polo fought in a war against Genoa. He was taken prisoner, and he told his cellmate of his travels. Later, the cellmate gathered the stories in a book called *The Travels of Marco Polo*. In this activity, children interview each other, taking turns pretending to be Marco Polo.

Materials:
Marco Polo Fact Cards (p. 12), Marco Polo Interview Sheet (p. 13), scissors, pens or pencils, books about Marco Polo

Preparation:
Gather books ahead of time.

Directions:
1. Divide the children into pairs.
2. Have each child learn at least three facts about Marco Polo.
3. The children then use their facts to write questions that their partner will ask them. For example, if a child found out that Marco Polo spent 24 years on his journey, the question might be, "How long did you spend traveling?"
4. Have the children take turns interviewing each other. One child plays Marco Polo, the other plays the interviewer. The interviewer asks the partner questions that he or she wrote down. The children then switch roles.

Option:
Have the children learn about different explorers and write interview questions and answers for each one.

Marco Polo Fact Cards

Marco Polo left Venice in 1271 to travel to China.

Marco Polo traveled with his father and uncle.

After 24 years traveling, Marco Polo returned to Venice in 1295.

Marco Polo was taken prisoner while Venice was at war with Genoa.

In his cell, Marco Polo told his cellmate about his travels.

Marco Polo's cellmate wrote a book called The Travels of Marco Polo.

Marco Polo Interview Sheet

My name is: _____

I learned these three facts about Marco Polo:

1. _____

   _____

   _____

2. _____

   _____

   _____

3. _____

   _____

   _____

Based on the facts that I learned, here are three questions
that I can answer about Marco Polo:

1. _____

   _____

2. _____

   _____

3. _____

How Many Silkworms?

This math activity can be used for different levels of mathematical study. For younger children, write a plus or minus on the piece of fabric in each equation. Write in a multiplication sign for older children.

Materials:
Silkworm Math (p. 15), pencils, crayons or markers

Preparation:
1. Fill in the missing signs (+, -, or x), then duplicate the Silkworm Math page. Make one for each child.
2. Make an answer key for self-checking, if desired.

Directions:
1. Give each child a copy of the Silkworm Math.
2. Have the children do the problems. They count the silkworms, see whether they are doing an addition, subtraction, or multiplication problem, then look at the numeral. They draw or write the correct number of silkworms after the equals sign.
3. Children can share their answers with the class. Or they can use the answer key for self-checking.

Options:
• For older children, pass out the Silkworm Math pages without any symbols written in the pieces of fabric. Let the children make their own problems to test their friends. They can add a +, -, or x and then write the answers on the back. Have the children trade papers.
• To make the problems more difficult, add more silkworms.

Silkworm Math

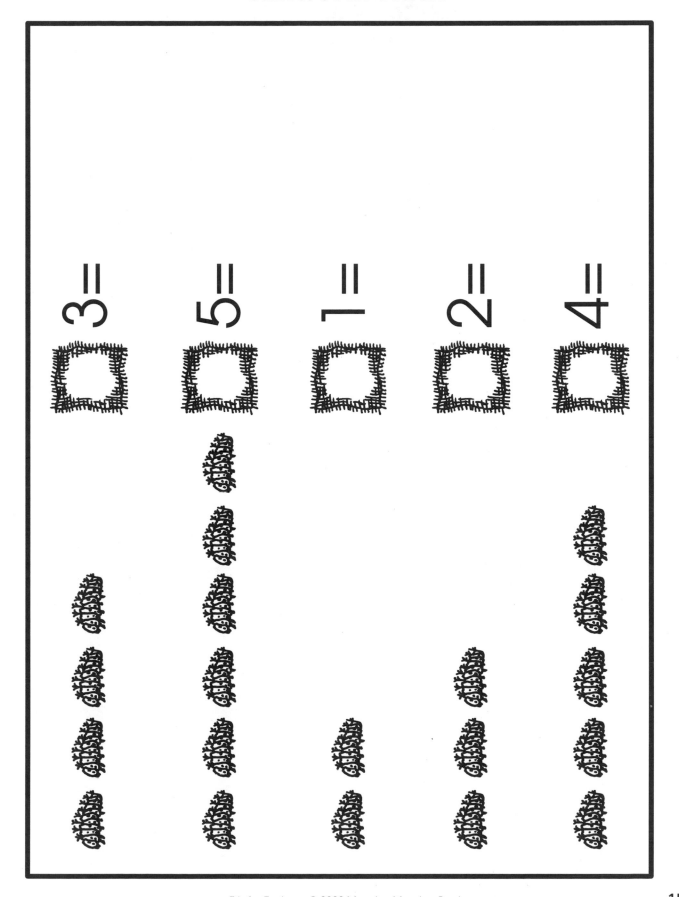

Marco Polo Spelling

A junk is a type of boat that the Polos used when sailing to Hormuz in what used to be Persia (now Iran). Sea-going junks had flat bottoms to carry cargo and square sails.

Materials:
Sails (p. 17), Junk (p. 18), bag, construction paper, scissors, colored markers, blue crepe paper, tape

Preparation:
1. Duplicate a copy of the spelling words for each child and one for teacher use.
2. Cut the words apart and color as desired.
3. Enlarge the junk pattern and post on a bulletin board. Create a crepe paper sea around it.

Directions:
1. Announce a date for a spelling "bee."
2. Divide the students into small groups. Have the children work together to learn the words. Let the children take the words home to study.
3. On the day of the spelling bee, put the spelling words in a bag. Pull one word from the bag at a time and have a child spell the word.
4. If the child spells the word correctly, he or she can post the sail on the junk. If not, another child tries to spell the word.
5. Continue until each child has a chance to spell one word and all of the sails are posted on the junk.

Options:
• Re-use words to let each child have a turn.
• White-out the given spelling words and write in other exploration-related words.

Sails

China

Explore

Fireworks

Junks

Khan

Ginger

Silkworm

Travel

Venice

Junk

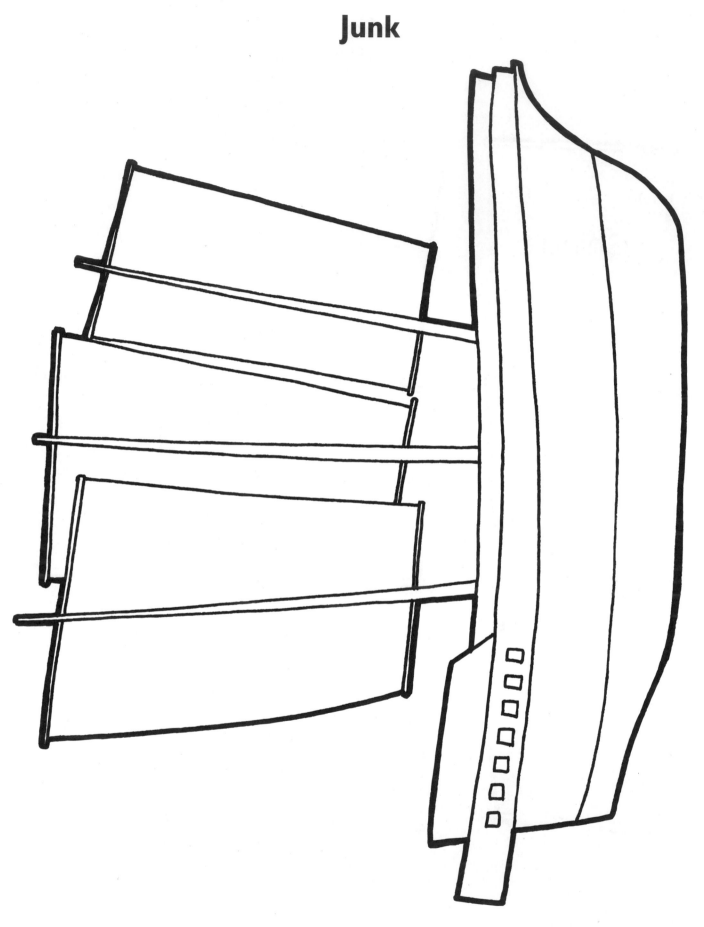

3-D Fireworks Display

You can make a large mural as a class using a large sheet of butcher paper, or have children make their own individual displays.

Materials:
Heavy construction paper, crayons or markers, tempera paint, shallow tins (for paint), paintbrushes, toothbrushes (to thumb-spray paint), decorative items (sequins, glitter, buttons), newsprint, colored chalk

Preparation:
Cover the workstation with newsprint, or do this activity outdoors.

Directions:
1. Explain that the children will be creating three-dimensional representations of fireworks, which Marco Polo saw on his travels to China.
2. Provide an assortment of colored paints, ribbons, tissue paper, shredded foil, and other decorative items for children to use to make their pictures.
3. Post the different pictures together on one bulletin board to create a grand "Fireworks Finale."

Option:
Have each child write a fact about Marco Polo and place it in the very center of the fireworks display.

Invention-tration

This concentration game will help children remember the different unique sights that Marco Polo saw on his journey.

Materials:
Concentration Cards (p. 21), crayons or markers, scissors, clear contact paper

Preparation:
1. For each game, make two copies of the patterns.
2. Color as desired, cover with clear contact paper for protection, and cut out.

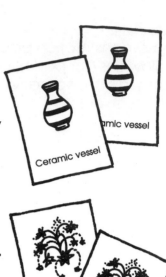

Directions:
1. To play the game, the players turn all of the cards face down. Then they take turns flipping two cards over. If the pictures on the cards match, they keep both and try again. If the cards don't match, they turn them face down and another child takes a turn.
2. The children can take the concentration game home to play with their families.

Option:
Children can make their own concentration cards featuring unusual sights seen by different explorers.

Concentration Cards

Fireworks	Coal
Ceramic vessel	Oil geyser
Silkworm	Woven silk fabric
Ginger plant	Paper money

Marco Polo Song

Marco Polo's Journey
(to the tune of "My Country 'Tis of Thee")

When he was just fifteen,
Marco went exploring.
On land, he roamed.
In the court of the Khan,
Where he was made welcome,
He stayed and worked so very long,
That he missed his home.

In the blink of an eye,
Twenty-four years went by,
Time to set sail.
He returned home again,
To see his kin and friends,
And share his news from start to end.
What a wondrous tale!

Personal Scrapbook

Have the children imagine that someone has journeyed to their neighborhood from far away, like Marco Polo did when he traveled to China.

Materials:
My Scrapbook (p. 24), pens or pencils, crayons or markers, scissors, staplers or hole punch and brads

Preparation:
Duplicate a copy of the patterns for each child.

Directions:
1. Give each child a scrapbook pattern to cut apart and collate with the cover on top.
2. Explain that the children will be looking around their neighborhoods for interesting sights. What might impress or astound someone who had never visited their area before?
3. When the children find items or objects that interest them, have the children draw pictures in their scrapbooks.
4. Ask the children to bring the books back to school to share with their friends.

Option:
Take the children on a walk through the neighborhood to look for interesting items around the school.

My
Scrapbook

E Is for Explorers © 2002 Monday Morning Books

A Flat, Flat World

In this activity, children will try to imagine what it was like to live in Columbus's time.

Materials:
Columbus Fact Cards (p. 26), books about Columbus, index cards, pens or pencils

Preparation:
1. Duplicate enough Columbus Fact Cards for children to share.
2. Gather books about Columbus.

Directions:
1. Divide the class into teams. Explain that one team will be arguing that the world is flat and the other that the world is round.
2. Have the children do research using the fact cards, books about the time of Columbus, or encyclopedias. They can also use their own ideas in the debate. Ask them prompting questions, such as why they might think that the world was flat.
3. Hold a classroom debate.

Option:
Have the children write their opinions in an editorial. Bring in several editorials from the local paper for the children to read first.

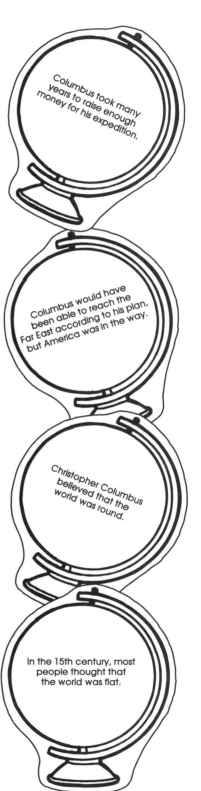

Columbus took many years to raise enough money for his expedition.

Columbus would have been able to reach the Far East according to his plan, but America was in the way.

Christopher Columbus believed that the world was round.

In the 15th century, most people thought that the world was flat.

Columbus Facts

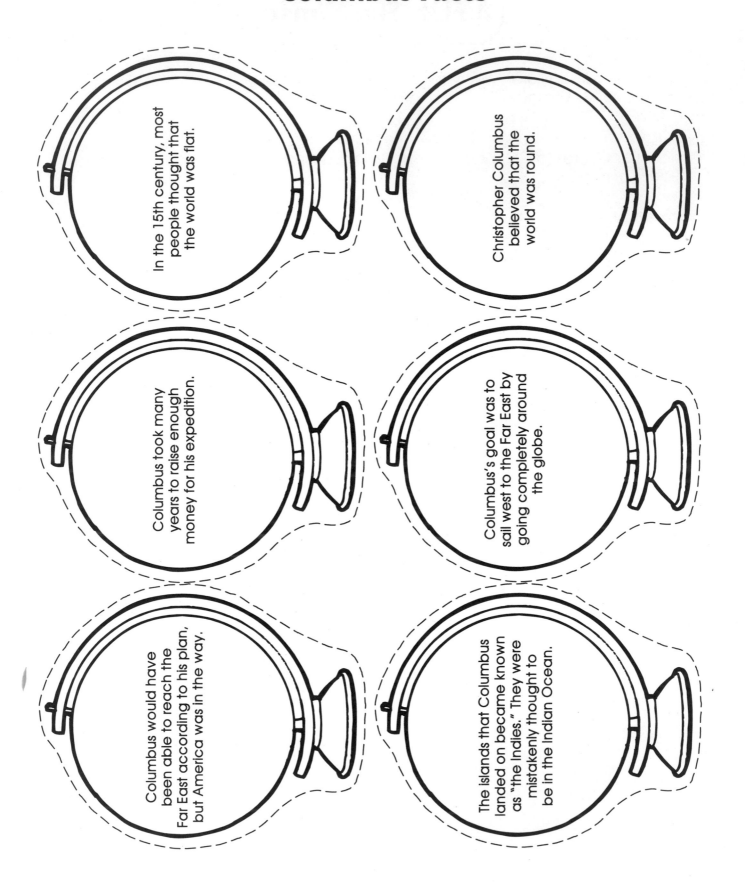

In the 15th century, most people thought that the world was flat.

Christopher Columbus believed that the world was round.

Columbus took many years to raise enough money for his expedition.

Columbus's goal was to sail west to the Far East by going completely around the globe.

Columbus would have been able to reach the Far East according to his plan, but America was in the way.

The islands that Columbus landed on became known as "the Indies." They were mistakenly thought to be in the Indian Ocean.

Spotting Sea Monsters

Many of the sailors on Columbus's ships believed that the seas were full of sea monsters. This activity will let the children use their imaginations!

Materials:
Paper, pens or pencils, crayons or markers

Preparation:
None

Directions:
1. Describe to the children the fears of Columbus's crew.
2. Have the children imagine that they were members of the crew, traveling to a distant land on a wondrous journey.
3. Have the children write short stories about what it might have been like to be a crew member. They can include facts and illustrate the stories with pictures.
4. Post the completed stories where other classes can read and enjoy them. Or bind the seafaring stories in a classroom book.

Facts to Share:
Spain's royalty gave Columbus three ships for his journey. Columbus captained the largest ship, called the *Santa Maria*. The *Nina* was a smaller ship, and the *Pinta* was similar in size to the *Nina*. Columbus set out on August 3, 1492. The lookout on the *Pinta* spotted land on October 12.

Across the Sea Math

This math activity can be used for different levels of mathematical study. For younger children, write in a plus or minus on the boats. Write in a multiplication sign for older children.

Materials:
Sea Supplies Math (p. 29), pencils, crayons or markers

Preparation:
1. Fill in the missing signs (+, -, or x), then duplicate the Sea Supplies Math page. Make one for each child.
2. Make an answer key for self-checking, if desired.

Directions:
1. Give each child a copy of Sea Supplies Math.
2. Have the children do the problems. They count the items in a line, look at the numeral, then see whether they are doing an addition, subtraction, or multiplication problem. They write their answer after the equals sign.
3. Children can share their answers with the class. Or they can use the answer key for self-checking.

Option:
For older children, pass out the math pages without any symbols written in the boats. Let the children make their own problems to test their friends. They can add a +, -, or x and then write the answers on the back. Have the children trade papers.

Sea Supplies Math

On Christopher Columbus's journey, the ships carried a large amount of supplies. These included live pigs, chickens, sacks of flour, rice, and water.

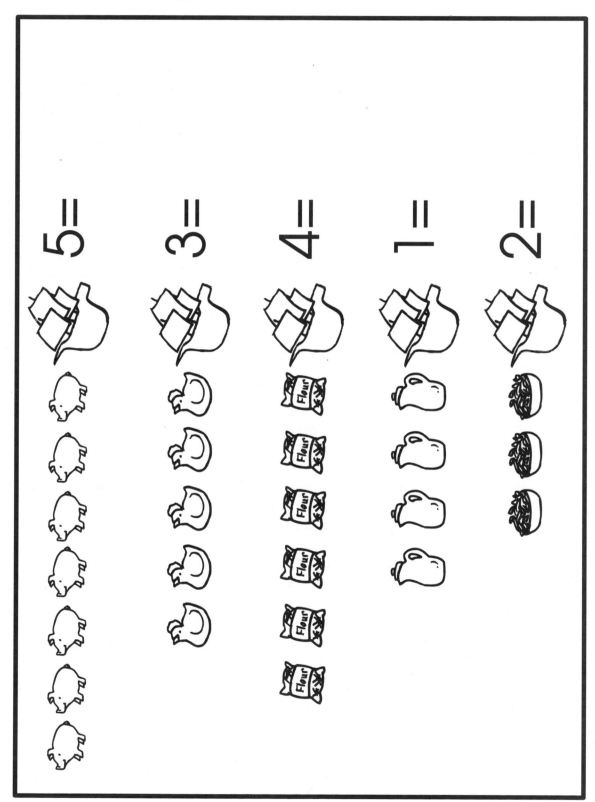

Sea Monster Spelling Bee

The words used in this spelling bee are terms that were important in Christopher Columbus's life.

Materials:
Sea Monsters (p. 31), scissors, crayons or markers, colored construction paper, tape

Preparation:
1. Duplicate a copy of the spelling word patterns for each child and one for teacher use.
2. Cut the spelling words apart and color as desired.
3. Create an ocean-themed bulletin board using blue construction paper.

Directions:
1. Announce a date for a spelling "bee."
2. Divide the students into small groups. Have the children work together to learn the words. Let the children take the spelling words home to study.
3. On the day of the spelling bee, put the words in a bag. Pull one word at a time from the bag, and have a child spell the word.
4. If the child spells the word correctly, he or she can post the word on the display. If not, another child tries to spell the word.
5. Continue until each child has a chance to spell one word, and all of the words are posted.

Option:
White-out the given spelling words and write in other exploration-related words.

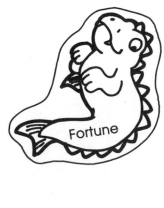

Sea Monsters

Spanish Shield

In the 16th century, a gold shield was made to commemorate Columbus's accomplishments. This shield, called The Allegory of Discovery, featured a variety of symbols including Neptune (the Greek sea god), a horn of plenty (to symbolize the natural resources found in America), and Columbus.

Materials:
Paper plates (one per child), crayons or markers

Preparation:
Create a shield on a paper plate to commemorate your own accomplishments.

Directions:
1. Discuss the Shield of Allegory with the children. Then explain that the children will be making shields to commemorate things that they've done that they are proud of.
2. Use your personal shield to demonstrate the activity.
3. Have the children use crayons or markers to decorate paper plates to look like shields.
4. When the children are finished, give each child a chance to share his or her shield with the rest of the class.

Option:
Have children use gold crayons or pens to do this activity.

Explorer Jeopardy

This game is played like the Jeopardy game show on television. However, in this case the children choose whether answers are true or false.

Materials:
Quiz Questions (p. 34), scissors, index cards, pencils, resource books about explorers

Preparation:
None

Directions:
1. Explain the game. You will read a statement. Children who think they know if the answer is true or false will raise their hands. Choose one child to answer.
2. Once the children understand the game, have each child create his or her own true/false question. The children should write the question on one side of an index card and the answer on the back. They can use information from this book, or from resource books about explorers and exploration.
3. Gather all of the children's questions and continue with the quiz game. Or let the children quiz each other.

Option:
Create a point system where questions are given a certain number of points based on the level of difficulty. Have a Final Jeopardy run-off between the children with the most points.

Explorer Jeopardy

6. When Columbus reached the islands off the coast of America, he thought he'd landed in China.

True

Explorer Jeopardy

3. King Ferdinand and Queen Isabella of Spain funded Columbus's expedition.

Explorer Jeopardy

1. Most people who lived in Columbus's time thought the world was round.

False

Explorer Jeopardy

7. The three ships that Spain provided for Columbus were called Marco Polo, Isabella, and Kublai Khan.

False

Quiz Questions

Explorer Jeopardy

1. Most people who lived in Columbus's time thought the world was round.

False

Explorer Jeopardy

2. Christopher Columbus sailed with forty ships.

False

Explorer Jeopardy

3. King Ferdinand and Queen Isabella of Spain funded Columbus's expedition.

True

Explorer Jeopardy

4. Sea monsters attacked Columbus's ships.

False

Explorer Jeopardy

5. Columbus proved the world was flat.

False

Explorer Jeopardy

6. When Columbus reached the islands off the coast of America, he thought he'd landed in China.

True

Explorer Jeopardy

7. The three ships that Spain provided for Columbus were called Marco Polo, Isabella, and Kublai Khan.

False

Explorer Jeopardy

It's a Round World, After All

It's a Round World, After All
(to the tune of "It's a Small World")

It's a round world, after all.
It's a round world, after all.
It's a round world, after all.
It's a round, round world.

When Columbus lived, people stood their ground.
And they said that the world was flat, not round.
They would not offer pay,
When Columbus would say,
It's a round world after all.

It's a round world, after all.
It's a round world, after all.
It's a round world, after all.
It's a round, round world.

Take a good long look at a rug or mat—
People thought the earth was as flat as that,
But Columbus, he planned
To prove to every man,
It's a round world, after all.

It's a round world, after all.
It's a round world, after all.
It's a round world, after all.
It's a round, round world.

So Columbus sailed, and he had a plan,
He'd prove what he knew to King Ferdinand,
He took his ships to sea
To show with honesty,
It's a round world after all.

Coat of Arms

In 1493, Christopher Columbus was given his own coat of arms. This gift was bestowed in honor of the discoveries he'd made.

Materials:
Coat of Arms Pattern (p. 37), pens or pencils, crayons or markers

Preparation:
Duplicate a copy of the Coat of Arms for each child.

Directions:
1. Give each child a Coat of Arms Pattern.
2. Have the children create their own coats of arms.
3. Post the completed pictures on a wall in the classroom.

Option:
Have the children create their coats of arms using fabric scraps, wallpaper samples, or other interesting materials.

E Is for Explorers © 2002 Monday Morning Books

Coat of Arms Pattern

Dictionary of Discovery

In 1804, Lewis and Clark led a team known as The Corps of Discovery on an exploration expedition. From St. Louis, they sailed up the Missouri River on their route to the Pacific Ocean. During their journey, they saw many unique and unusual plants and animals.

Materials:
Discovery Patterns (p. 39), construction paper, hole punch, yarn or brads, scissors, crayons or markers, glue or paste

Preparation:
Duplicate a copy of the Discovery Patterns for each child.

Directions:
1. Explain that the students will be pretending that they were members of The Corps of Discovery led by Lewis and Clark.
2. Using the Discovery Patterns, they will create picture dictionaries, featuring the different sights seen by the corps, as well as some of the items that the corps brought with them.
3. Children can use the patterns or draw their own pictures based on facts they find in encyclopedias or other books.
4. Have the children create picture dictionaries on sheets of construction paper bound together with brads or yarn.

Option:
Work as a class to create a large picture dictionary.

E Is for Explorers © 2002 Monday Morning Books

Discovery Patterns

On their expedition, Lewis and Clark brought medicines, food supplies, and presents to give to the Native Americans.

Corps of Discovery Letters

Writing letters is one way to strengthen a child's language skills.

Materials:
Lewis and Clark Fact Cards (p. 41), scissors, paper, pens or pencils

Preparation:
Duplicate enough fact cards for the children to share.

Directions:
1. Have the children imagine that they were members of the Corps of Discovery. With this assignment, they will write to their relatives back home about their experiences.
2. Provide Lewis and Clark Fact Cards, as well as books about the expedition and encyclopedias, for the children to use for research.
3. Each child can write a letter or postcard that includes several facts about the expedition.

Option:
Post the letters on a Corps of Discovery bulletin board.

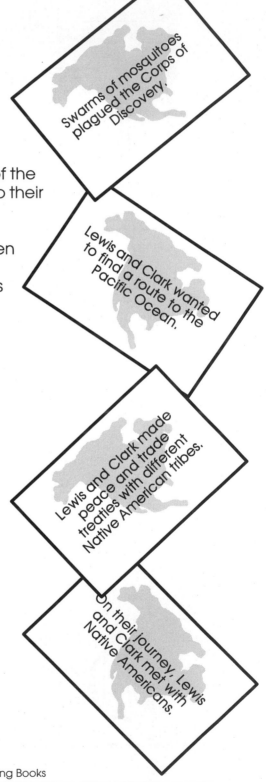

Swarms of mosquitoes plagued the Corps of Discovery.

Lewis and Clark wanted to find a route to the Pacific Ocean.

Lewis and Clark made peace and trade treaties with different Native American tribes.

On their journey, Lewis and Clark met with Native Americans.

Lewis and Clark Fact Cards

Lewis and Clark wanted to find a route to the Pacific Ocean.

Swarms of mosquitoes plagued the Corps of Discovery.

On their journey, Lewis and Clark met with Native Americans.

Lewis and Clark made peace and trade treaties with different Native American tribes.

The team of 30 men who traveled with Lewis and Clark were known as the Corps of Discovery.

The Corps of Discovery began in St. Louis. They left on May 14, 1804.

Lewis and Clark were helped on their journey by a member of the Shoshoni tribe named Sacagewea.

On November 7, Lewis and Clark saw the Pacific Ocean.

How Many Mosquitoes?

On the journey, the Corps of Discovery was bothered by mosquitoes during the night and day. Lewis complained both about the weather and the mosquito swarms.

This math activity can be used for different levels of mathematical study. For younger children, write a plus or minus sign on each equation. Write in a multiplication sign for older children.

Materials:
Mosquito Math (p. 43), pencils, crayons or markers

Preparation:
1. Fill in the missing signs (+, -, or x), then duplicate the Mosquito Math page. Make one for each child.
2. Make an answer key for self-checking, if desired.

Directions:
1. Give each child a copy of Mosquito Math.
2. Have the children do the problems. They count the mosquitoes, see whether they are doing an addition, subtraction, or multiplication problem, then look at the numeral. They draw the correct number of mosquitoes, or the correct numeral, after the equals sign.
3. Children can share their answers with the class. Or they can use the answer key for self-checking.

Options:
• For older children, pass out the Mosquito Math pages without any symbols written in the boxes. Let the children make their own problems to test their friends. They can add a +, -, or x and then write the answers on the back. Have the children trade papers.
• To make the problems more difficult, add more mosquitoes.

Mosquito Math

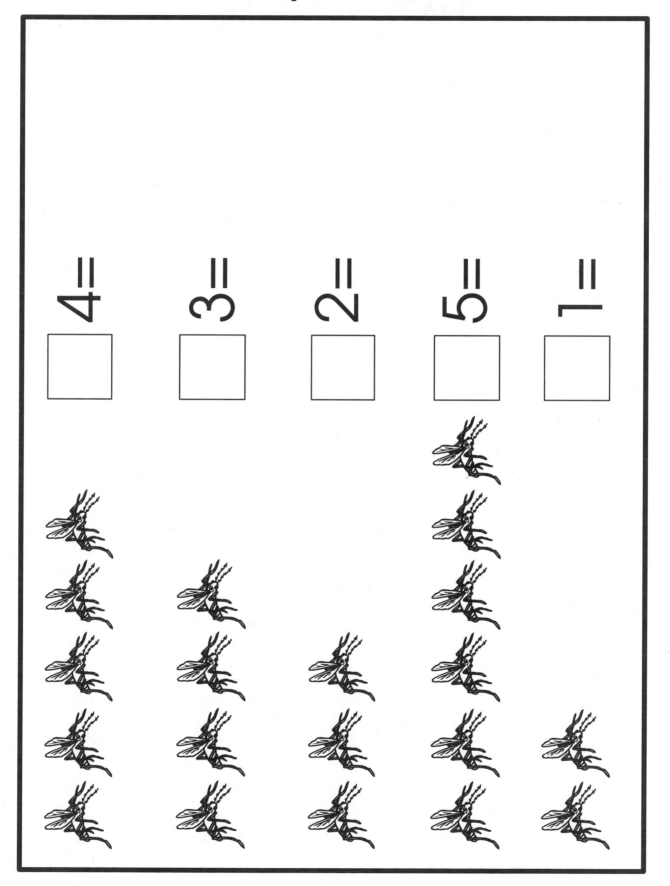

Log Fort Spelling

Lewis and Clark spent their winter in an area that is now part of North Dakota. To weather the winter, they set up camp and built a log fort.

Materials:
Logs (p. 45), Log Cabin (p. 46), bag, construction paper, scissors, colored markers, tape

Preparation:
1. Duplicate a copy of the Logs for each child and one for teacher use.
2. Cut one set of the Logs apart and color as desired.
3. Duplicate the Log Cabin and post on a bulletin board.

Directions:
1. Announce a date for a spelling "bee."
2. Divide the students into small groups. Have the children work together to learn the words. Let the children take the words home to study.
3. On the day of the spelling bee, put the spelling patterns in a bag. Pull one pattern from the bag at a time and have a child spell the word.
4. If the child spells the word correctly, he or she can post the log on the cabin. If not, another child tries to spell the word.
5. Continue until each child has a chance to spell one word, and all of the logs are posted on the board.

Option:
Use the blank logs to make enough words for each child in the classroom to spell at least one. Or re-use words to let each child have a turn.

E Is for Explorers © 2002 Monday Morning Books

Logs

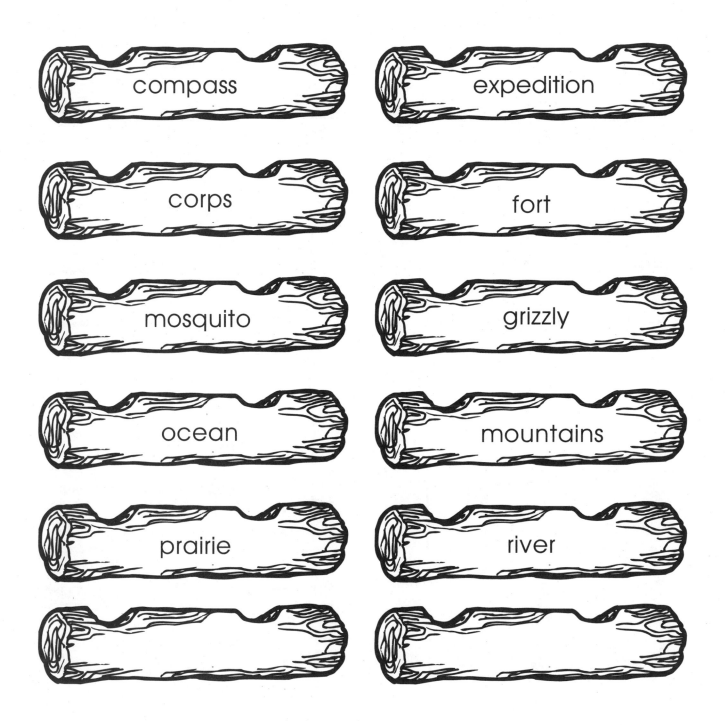

compass

expedition

corps

fort

mosquito

grizzly

ocean

mountains

prairie

river

Log Cabin

Carrying a Compass

Lewis and Clark brought many items with them on their journey. These included gifts to use to make peace with the Native Americans, air guns, and Clark's pocket compass.

Materials:
Compass Patterns (p. 48), scissors, heavy paper, paper clips, crayons or markers, pens or pencils, paste or glue

Preparation:
Duplicate a Compass Pattern for each child.

Directions:
1. Give each child a compass to cut out.
2. Have the children cut squares from heavy paper that are slightly larger than the compass patterns.
3. The children glue the compass to the squares and then color both as desired.
4. Provide paper clips for the children to use to make chains for their compasses.
5. Help the children poke holes in the paper squares and attach their chains.

Option:
Bring in a real working compass for the children to observe.

Compass Patterns

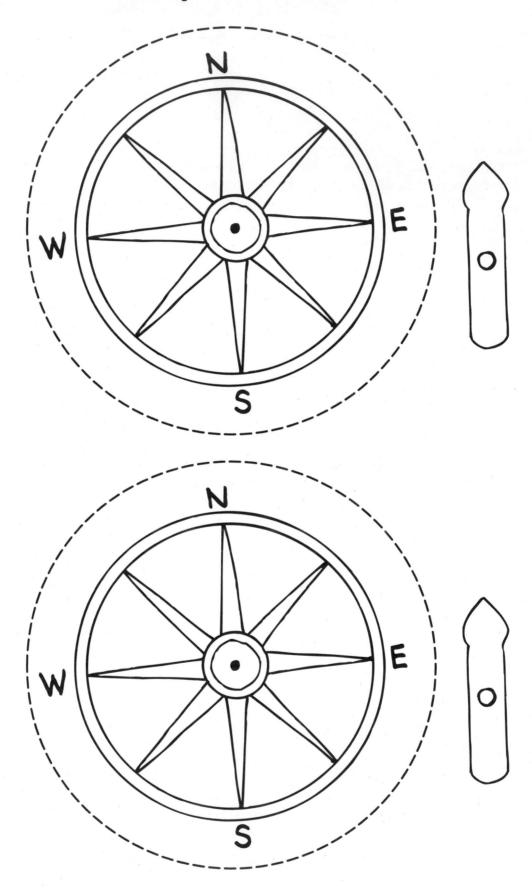

E Is for Explorers © 2002 Monday Morning Books

Lewis and Clark Concentration

This activity uses items seen and carried on the Corps of Discovery expedition in the standard concentration game.

Materials:
Discovery Patterns (p. 39), heavy paper, crayons or markers, envelopes (one per child)

Preparation:
Duplicate two copies of the patterns for each child.

Directions:
1. Give each child two copies of the patterns to color, cut out, and glue to heavy paper. Have the children then cut the paper to make cards.
2. Teach the children the concentration game, or remind them of the rules. They turn all of the cards face down. Then they take turns flipping two cards over. If the pictures on the cards match, they keep both and try again. If the cards don't match, they turn them face down and another child takes a turn.
3. The children can take the concentration game home to play with their families.

Option:
Children can make their own cards using their own drawings.

Sacagewea Song

Sacagewea Song
(to the tune of "Home on the Range")

The journey was hard,
It was both long and far.
Yes, we needed some help right away.
A guide through the land,
Who could lend us a hand,
And we found one named Sacagewea.

She guided with class,
And she showed us the famed Lemhi Pass.
With her help and her aid,
We went out on our way,
And we found the Pacific, at last.

E Is for Explorers © 2002 Monday Morning Books

Designing Coins

Lewis and Clark were surprised by the height of the Rocky Mountains. Luckily, they had help. Sacagewea, the Shoshoni Indian wife of a Canadian interpreter, helped Lewis and Clark by showing them the Lemhi Pass and guiding them towards the Columbia River.

Materials:
Paper plates, crayons or markers

Preparation:
None

Directions:
1. Explain to the children that the United States honored Sacagewea with a dollar coin.
2. Have the children think about who they might want to honor, either an explorer, someone from the Lewis and Clark expedition, or someone they know.
3. Give each child a paper plate to take home. Have the children work at home to design coins honoring the people of their choice.
4. Have the children bring the coins back to share with the class.

Option:
Post the finished paper plates on a classroom bulletin board.

Note: There are a variety of spellings of Sacagewea, including with a "j" instead of a "g."

Moon Mural

Children may not realize that some of the most exciting explorers were space pioneers. Children will learn about them, and other astronauts, as they create a moon mural display.

Materials:
Astro Fact Cards (p. 53), lined paper, pens or pencils, paper plates (one per child), crayons, butcher paper, tempera paint, paintbrushes

Preparation:
Duplicate a copy of the cards for each child.

Directions:
1. Explain that the children will be doing research about astronauts.
2. Provide a variety of resources, including encyclopedias, books about the space journey, and Astro Fact Cards.
3. Have the children write brief reports about astronauts.
4. Give each child a paper plate to decorate to look like the moon.
5. Have each child post his or her report in the center of a plate.
6. Working together, the children can create a space mural on butcher paper.
7. When the mural is dry, have the children post their moon reports on the mural.

Option
Instead of creating moons, the children could write their reports on other space-related shapes, including stars, planets, comets, rockets, and so on.

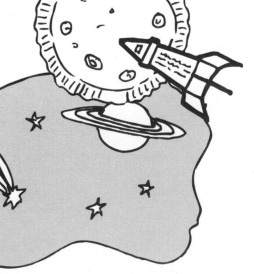

E Is for Explorers © 2002 Monday Morning Books

Astro Fact Cards

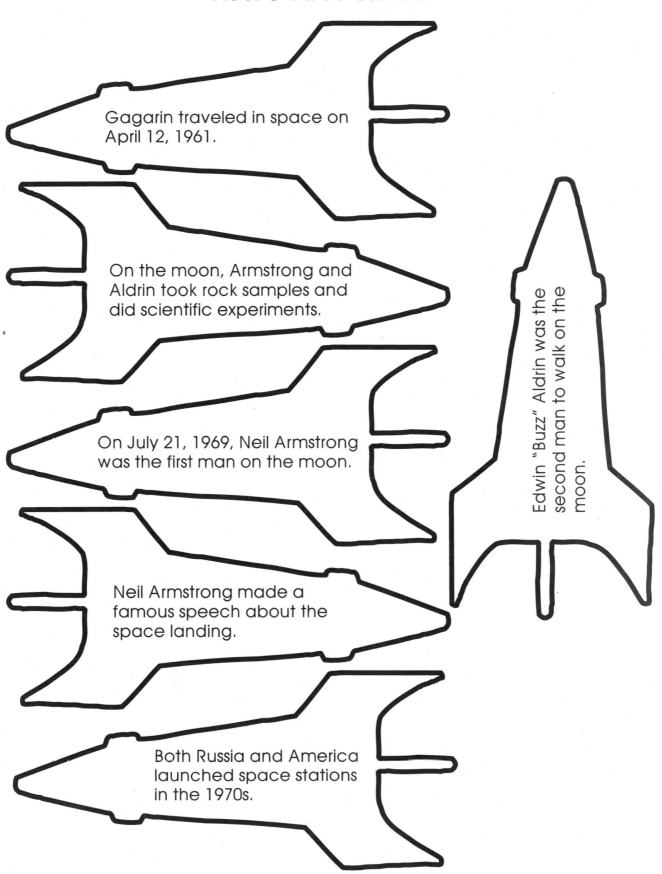

Gagarin traveled in space on April 12, 1961.

On the moon, Armstrong and Aldrin took rock samples and did scientific experiments.

On July 21, 1969, Neil Armstrong was the first man on the moon.

Neil Armstrong made a famous speech about the space landing.

Both Russia and America launched space stations in the 1970s.

Edwin "Buzz" Aldrin was the second man to walk on the moon.

Space Trading Cards

Children will create trading cards featuring illustrations and facts about space travel.

Materials:
Space Cards (p. 55), space exploration resources, index cards cut in half, paper, pens or pencils, crayons or markers, scissors

Preparation:
1. Duplicate a copy of the cards for each child.
2. Gather space-related books for children to use.

Directions:
1. Give each child a copy of the cards to color and cut apart.
2. Explain that the children will be making their own trading cards. Have the children choose a subject to research. (They can use the items on the cards, or come up with their own ideas.)
3. Have the children use books or the Web to find facts.
4. If the children are using the space exploration cards, they can simply write facts on the backs. If making their own cards, the children can draw a picture on one side of an index card and a fact on the back.
5. The children can then trade cards.

Options:
• Younger children can use the cards to play a game of concentration. Duplicate two copies of the cards for each game.
• Older children can add facts to their pictures.

Space Exploration Cards

Man on the Moon Math

This math activity is drawn from Neil Armstrong's famous, "One small step" speech. It can be used for different levels of mathematical study. For younger children, write a plus or minus sign in each equation. Write in a multiplication sign for older children.

Materials:
How Many Steps? (p. 57), pencils, crayons or markers

Preparation:
1. Fill in the missing signs (+, -, or x), then duplicate the math page. Make one for each child.
2. Make an answer key for self-checking, if desired.

Directions:
1. Give each child a copy of the math page.
2. Have the children do the problems. They count the steps, see whether they are doing an addition, subtraction, or multiplication problem, then look at the numeral. They write in the answer after the equals sign.
3. Children can share their answers with the class. Or they can use the answer key for self-checking.

Option:
For older children, pass out the math pages without any symbols written in the flags. Let the children make their own problems to test their friends. They can add a +, -, or x and then write the answers on the back. Have the children trade papers.

E Is for Explorers © 2002 Monday Morning Books

How Many Steps?

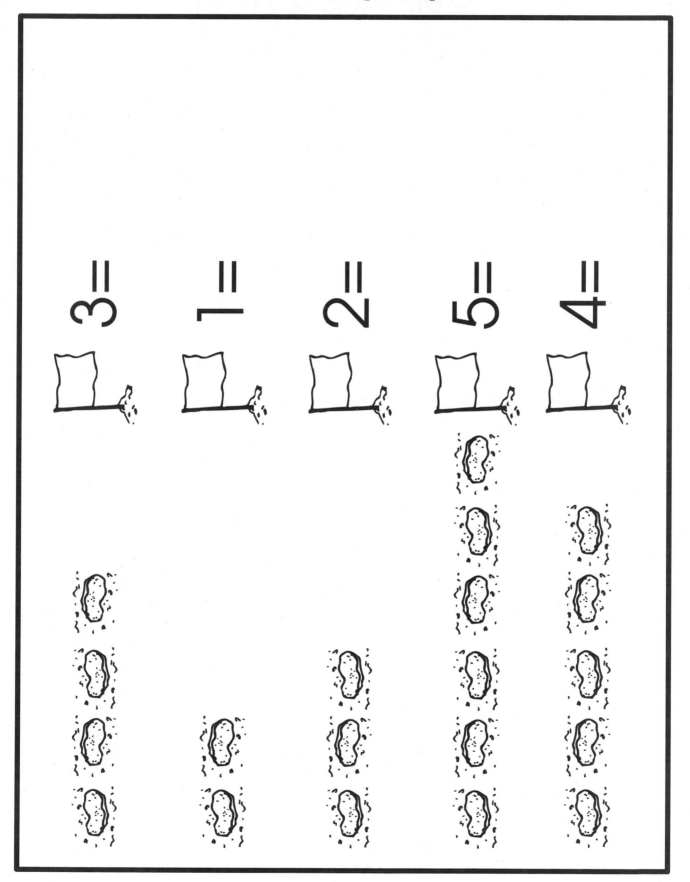

To the Moon Spelling

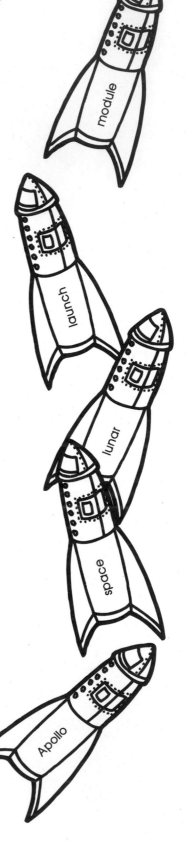

This activity will allow children to participate in creating a large, cooperative mobile to feature the spelling patterns.

Materials:
Rocket Patterns (p. 59), bag, hole punch, hanger, crayons or markers, scissors, yarn or string

Preparation:
1. Duplicate a copy of the patterns for each child and one for teacher use.
2. Cut one set of the patterns apart and color as desired. Punch a hole in each one and tie a length of yarn through the hole.
3. Bend a wire hanger to create a frame for a mobile.

Directions:
1. Announce a date for a spelling "bee."
2. Divide the students into small groups. Have the children work together to learn the words. Let the children take the words home to study.
3. On the day of the spelling bee, put the words in a bag. Pull one word from the bag at a time and have a child spell the word.
4. If the child spells the word correctly, he or she can tie the pattern to the hanger.
5. Continue until each child has a chance to spell one word and the mobile is complete.

Option:
White-out the words on the patterns and write in other space-related spelling words.

Rocket Patterns

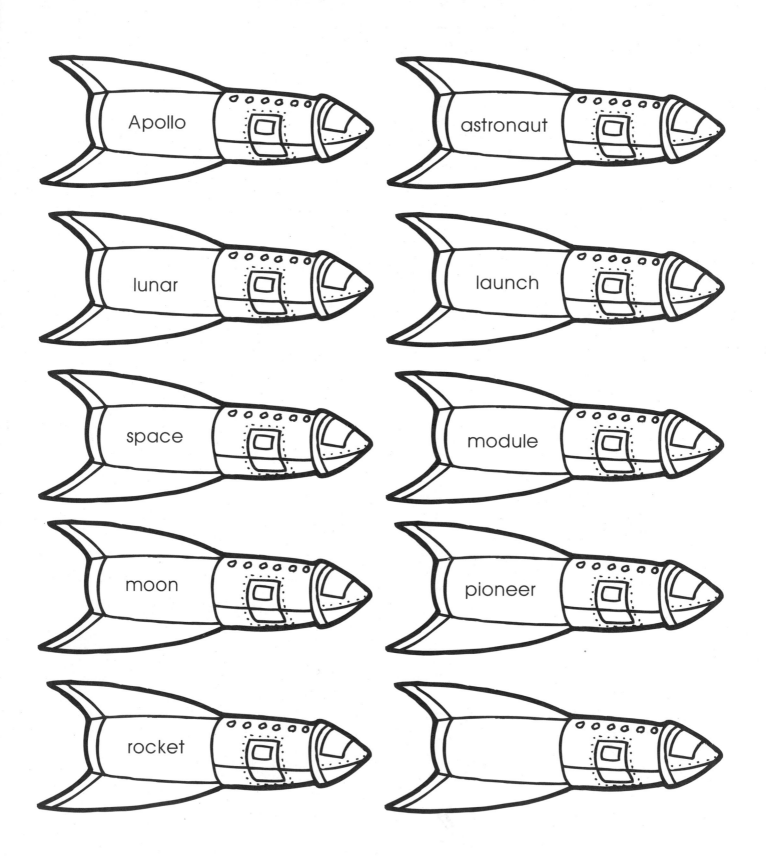

Apollo

astronaut

lunar

launch

space

module

moon

pioneer

rocket

One Small Step...

Neil Armstrong took one small step for man, and one large step for mankind. Your students can take one small step for the future.

Materials:
Tempera paint, butcher paper, shallow tins (for paint), newsprint

Preparation:
Cover the workstation with newsprint. (Consider doing this activity outdoors.)

Directions:
1. Discuss the first steps that Neil Armstrong made on the moon. If possible, show televised footage or share photographic images from newspapers of the time.
2. Explain that the children will be making art depicting the "one small step."
3. Provide tins of colored paint and have the children, one at a time, make footprints on the butcher paper. They should use different colors and create a unique design.
4. When the paper is dry, post it in the classroom to commemorate the moon landing.

Option:
Do this activity with plaster of Paris and let each child keep his or her own "small step."

E Is for Explorers © 2002 Monday Morning Books

Who Wants to be an Explorer?

Children will challenge each other with multiple-choice questions to share what they know about exploration

Materials:
Index cards, pencils, resource books about exploration

Preparation:
None

Directions:
1. Have each child create his or her own question about explorers with four possible answers. The children should write the question and answers on one side of an index card and the correct answer on the back. They can use information from this book, or from resource books about explorers. Be sure to explain that three of the answers should be incorrect and only one will be correct.
2. Gather all of the children's questions and stage a quiz game. Or let the children quiz each other.

Options:
• Let the children have a chance to remove two incorrect answers.
• Allow children to confer with a friend about the correct answer.

Space Song

One Small Step
(to the tune of "On Top of Old Smokey")

All dressed in a space suit,
With "Buzz" at his side,
Neil Armstrong took one step,
That now famous stride.

A large step for mankind,
A small step for man,
Neil Armstrong's first moon walk
Took years to be planned.

Away from Apollo,
And out into space
Neil Armstrong took one step
For the human race.

Whenever you're faced with
A problem that's grand.
Remember that small step
Was how it began.

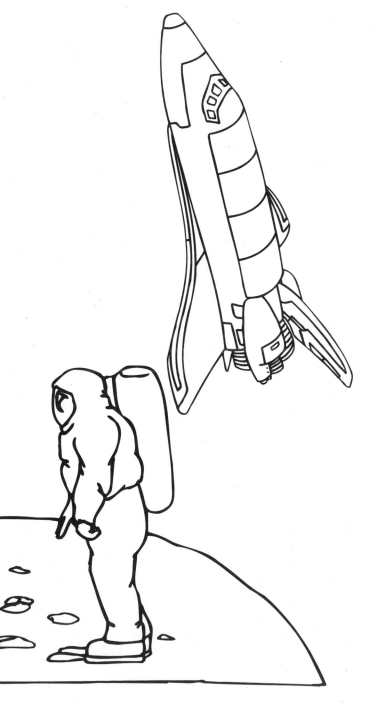

E Is for Explorers © 2002 Monday Morning Books

Astronaut Bookmark

Children will use this bookmark to keep track of the different space-related materials that they read.

Materials:
Bookmark (this page), crayons or markers, scissors

Preparation:
Duplicate a copy of the bookmark for each child.

Directions:
1. Have the children cut out and color the book mark.
2. Explain that each time the children read a book, they should write the title on the bookmark.
3. When the children finish the bookmark, they can make their own to continue to track their reading.

Option:
Have the children make bookmarks for their friends.

Explorer Diploma

Name

HAS MASTERED

THE CONCEPT OF

EXPLORATION

AND IS AN HONORARY EXPLORER

HONORARY EXPLORER